# HOW TO HANDLE
# PERSECUTION

## BY
## JOHN MACARTHUR

**SCAN THIS CODE** WITH YOUR SMARTPHONE
OR OTHER DEVICE TO FOLLOW
ALONG WITH THE SERMON AUDIO.

ISBN: 978-1-955292-07-8

Printed in the United States of America

Valencia, California

# CONTENTS

HOW TO HANDLE PERSECUTION,                1
PART 1


HOW TO HANDLE PERSECUTION,                27
PART 2


THE PERSECUTED CHURCH                     53
REACHES OUT


HOW TO TURN PERSECUTION                   79
INTO PRODUCTION

# HOW TO HANDLE
# PERSECUTION,
## PART 1

## INTRODUCTION

### A. The Persecution of Christians

1. Observed

Persecution is an intrinsic part of Christianity. In Acts 4:1–32 are some tremendous insights that we can learn from the way the apostles handled persecution. For the early church, persecution was a blessing. That is still true today—persecution is a blessing to all churches and all believers. There were five organized efforts within eleven years to persecute the church in Jerusalem. Acts 4 records the beginnings of those efforts. They were really the beginning of all the persecution that the church has endured for nearly two thousand years.

Persecution is subtler today than in the past, when Christians could expect fierce, inhumane physical attacks for their faith. Today, Satan targets the intangible self more than the physical—you may not lose your head, but you may lose your job, standing, or opportunities. The heroism of uncompromising Christian martyrs inspired many in the early days of the church, but the quiet complacency and compromise of so many today to social and psychological pressures has far more effectively gutted the church of spiritual vitality. The greatest persecutor of evangelical Christianity is probably liberal Christianity. Satan is spiritually killing the contemporary church without physically having to kill anybody in it by inducing it to be complacent, indolent, fat, rich, and socially oriented. The church has watered down its theology to accommodate the world. Satan's present assault may be less obvious, but it is in fact more deadly.

## 2. Anticipated

### a. Expecting persecution

In John 15, Jesus warned His disciples to expect persecution. He said, "If the world hates you, you know that it has hated Me before it hated you. If you were of the world, the world would love its own" (vv. 18–19). That's why John wrote, "Do not love the world nor the things in the world" (1 John 2:15). The Christian who loves the world has played perfectly into Satan's scheme—he no longer confronts the world in any way, and thus nullifies his effectiveness for the gospel even more than if he'd been killed.

Christ continued, "If you were of the world, the world would love its own; but because you are not of the world, but I chose you out of the world, because of this the world hates you. Remember the word that I said to you, 'A slave is not greater than his master.' If they persecuted Me, they will also persecute you" (John 15:19–20). Also, "They will make you outcasts from the synagogue, but an hour is coming for everyone who kills you to think that he is offering service to God" (16:2).

Peter echoed that warning in 1 Peter 2:21: "You have been called for this purpose, since Christ also suffered for you, leaving you an example for you to follow in His steps." When you confront the world, it will react violently. Some people succumb to Satan's persecution in order to avoid the world's hostility, but Paul told Timothy, "All who desire to live

godly in Christ Jesus will be persecuted" (2
Tim. 3:12).

b. Avoiding persecution

If you're a Christian and not suffering
persecution, you may need to examine
whether you truly "live godly in Christ."
It may be that you have hidden your true
identity in public and are so conformed to
your environment that you bear no notable
difference to it. But if you live as God
intends, openly and holy in the world, you
will inevitably clash with Satan. You will
be a living rebuke to his world system, and
persecution will inevitably follow.

## B. The Perseverance of Christians

### 1. Confronting unbelievers

If you live a godly life, unbelievers may be drawn
to you initially. But unless they come to Christ,
how you live will repel them as they find out
more about you.

That happened with the early church. Acts 2:47
tells us that people looked favorably upon them.
In Acts 3 people flocked to Peter and John upon
witnessing them heal a lame man just outside
the Temple (vv. 1–11). Peter then powerfully
preached to them that Jesus was the Messiah
and indicted Israel for executing Him (vv. 12–

26). Peter closed with an invitation that began, "Repent therefore and be converted, that your sins may be blotted out" (v. 19, NKJV). Right where people were performing their religious duties, Peter confronted the error of their worship.

That's the kind of confrontation that brings hostility from the world—the kind that God requires of us. We are not to hide so that we can protect our name, ego, or status among unbelievers.

2. Converting unbelievers

Note the result of Peter's preaching: "Many of those who had heard the message believed" (4:4). You may evade immediate suffering by hiding your allegiance to Christ, but you'll also fail those who need you to bring the gospel to them. Our lives are expendable for the sake of others.

Acts 4:4 continues, "And the number of the men came to be about five thousand." There are two Greek words for "man": *anthropos*, which means mankind, generally; and *andros*, which means specifically male, as opposed to female. Acts 4:4 uses the latter word. And it's fair to suppose that at least five thousand women and children accompanied the five thousand men who were saved, so the early church began suddenly and began large. That was how God chose to work through Peter's boldness for the gospel of Christ.

## I. THE PERSECUTION MANIFEST (ACTS 4:1–4)

### A. The Arrest Initiated (v. 1)

"As they were speaking to the people, the priests and the captain of the temple guard and the Sadducees came up to them . . ."

The crowd in the Temple courtyard had witnessed the lame man's healing, so they eagerly listened to Peter. Verse 2 says that that "greatly disturbed" this contingent of Temple officials and religious leaders, so they arrested Peter and John.

1. By the priests

The priests were supposed to represent God, but the fact that they wanted to stop Peter from preaching shows how far removed from God the priesthood had become. There were so many priests that they were divided into twenty-four courses and selected only by lot to serve at a given time; surely this group had waited eagerly for their week to minister and did not welcome the apostles' disturbance. They presented the religious opposition to the church. In fact, it's still often true that persecution of Christians arises from other religious groups, including Judaism.

2. By the captain of the Temple

The captain of the Temple was its head of police. Political opposition still faces the church in many parts of the world today, like China and Russia. And while Rome was very tolerant of its subjugated people, it was merciless toward public disorder. The last thing this captain wanted was a riot.

3. By the Sadducees

The Sadducees combined the worst of Israel's religious and political opposition in their persecution of the church. They were theological liberals, and all high priests of the period were Sadducees. They were the opposition party to the Pharisees. The Pharisees' antagonism to Christ dominates the gospels, while the Sadducees' dominates Acts.

Unlike the Pharisees, the Sadducees tended to be extremely wealthy due to their collaboration with Rome. They kept on friendly terms with the empire in order to maintain their prestige, power, and comforts. Though a minority within Israel, the Sadducees were its dominant political party.

They viewed religion as merely a social custom. Specifically, they rejected Judaism's rabbinical laws, they repudiated God's sovereignty in favor of man's volition, and they denied the existence of the afterlife, angels, and the spirit world.

## B. The Anxiety Indicated (v. 2)

". . . being greatly disturbed because they were teaching the people and proclaiming in Jesus the resurrection from the dead."

Acts 4:2 gives us the clear reason these high-ranking men of Jerusalem went after Peter and John. Notice they were "greatly disturbed," or "thoroughly pained." Their mental anguish was rooted in indignation and wrath. The same Greek word appears in Acts 16:18, where Paul was provoked over the Philippian woman who was under the power of an evil spirit. That was the response of the priests, the Sadducees, and the Temple captain to Peter and John for three reasons:

1. They doubted the competency of the preachers

These community leaders believed they had the corner on all truth and that only they had the right to teach. In their eyes, Peter and John had no prerogative to do so, much less in the Temple and on matters that contradicted the leaders' own teachings.

They also disdained Peter and John as unqualified to teach. "As they observed the confidence of Peter and John and understood that they were uneducated and untrained men, they were amazed" (v. 13).

a. "Uneducated"

Peter and John weren't formally versed in Jewish theology and rabbinic law; they hadn't been to the proper schools. The same accusation had been leveled at Jesus, who demonstrated that His teaching came not from their institutions but from God (cf. John 12:49–50).

b. "Untrained"

Peter and John were laypeople, unschooled amateurs from a despised, backwater town who impudently dared contradict these leaders and their whole system, in their own house.

2. They disliked the core of the preaching

That Peter and John preached Jesus also angered the Temple officials and religious leaders. They had declared Jesus a blasphemer, but Peter denounced the whole nation of Israel for murdering Him, their own Messiah (Acts 3:13–15). To this day, no Jewish congregation would welcome that message.

3. They denied the condemnation in the preaching

Finally, the religious leaders could not accept Peter and John's "teaching . . . in Jesus the resurrection from the dead" (v. 2). A resurrected Jesus proved the Jews had been wrong about Him and were subject to condemnation.

Their hearts must have condemned them for their hypocrisy, but that did not halt their determination to silence these preachers of truth. Recall also that the Sadducees did not believe in resurrection at all. The apostles' teaching would have particularly outraged them.

## C. The Apostles Imprisoned (v. 3)

"And they laid hands on them and put them in jail until the next day, for it was already evening."

Peter and John had come to the Temple around 3 p.m. for the afternoon prayers (3:1) and remained until "evening," around 6 p.m., before the Jewish officials arrested and jailed them overnight. This was the beginning of the persecution of the church.

## D. The Audience Influenced (v. 4)

"But many of those who had heard the message believed; and the number of the men came to be about five thousand."

But imprisoning the apostles didn't nullify their effect; it didn't stop the spread of the gospel. Instead, it was the first incident of many through which persecution has led to the church's growth rather than its destruction. Personal trials are God's way of maturing the Christian (Jas. 1:2–4), and church-wide persecution is how He matures His church.

# HOW PERSECUTION
# PROMPTS GROWTH

Persecution always results in spiritual growth. It strips the tares out of the church (Matt. 13:24–26). Those who merely profess to know and love the Lord will abandon the church as soon as persecution sets in, because false faith is ultimately unwilling to pay the price of following Christ. Prosperity preachers and charismatic charlatans will bolt the moment their deceptions are no longer lucrative; others will flee the church as soon as their professed commitments become inconvenient. Persecution purifies the church and thereby actually increases the church's effectiveness.

It would be cavalier and foolish to pray for the persecution of the church, or to intentionally incite the opposition of the world—the truth of God's Word provides all the provocation they need. What we need to remember, from the testimony of both Scripture and church history, is that God has never forgotten or overlooked His people in their suffering. In fact, we can know that He is working in the midst of even the fiercest persecution to purge and preserve His true church.

## II. THE PERSECUTION MET (ACTS 4:3, 5–32)

We can identify seven practical principles for meeting persecution in Acts 4. They all exist in the important context of committing yourself to confronting the world in order to evangelize it—and knowing that that will provoke persecution, but will also facilitate your personal growth and fulfill your purpose for existing in the world. James 1:2 says, "Consider it all joy, my brethren, when you encounter various trials." We can face persecution with great joy for righteousness' sake (cf. Matt. 5:10).

### A. Be Submissive in Persecution (vv. 3, 5–7)

#### 1. The apostles' example of submission

In Acts 4:3 Peter and John were taken into custody. Verses 5–7 say, "On the next day, their rulers and elders and scribes were gathered together in Jerusalem; and Annas the high priest was there, and Caiaphas and John and Alexander, and all who were of high-priestly descent. When they had placed [Peter, John, and the healed man] in the center, they began to inquire, 'By what power, or in what name, have you done this?'" Peter and John did not offer any resistance; they did not strike back at their arresters or start a brawl. Neither did they lose heart and develop a martyr's complex of lying down to die. They simply trusted God. They had been obedient to proclaim Christ, and they saw their persecution as a great opportunity from Him, trusting that even under arrest they were where God wanted them.

If in the course of obeying the Lord you end up in difficult circumstances, you can be confident that God ordained that outcome for your good. This is not you ending up in trouble due to your own disobedience (1 Pet. 2:20). But when you're faithful, even pain cannot take your peace. When persecuted for the gospel, praise God and don't fight back.

2. The apostles' encounter with the Sanhedrin

    a. Introduction to the Sanhedrin

    Verse 5 shows us the Sanhedrin, the "rulers and elders and scribes" of Israel—its Supreme Court. Even under Rome, the Sanhedrin had the right to arrest people. Seventy-one men altogether made up that council, including the high priest at its head; the scribes were experts in the law, the elders from among the people, and the remaining members from the priestly family. They were a mixed group, at best.

    "Annas the high priest" (v. 6) was a Sadducee and former high priest that Rome had deposed, but who still controlled things behind the scenes. In fact upon His arrest, Jesus was immediately taken to Annas (John

18:12–13), the most powerful man in Israel.

Caiaphas, Annas's son-in-law, was the high priest Rome had appointed, and he was as bad as Annas. Then Acts 4:6 mentions two councilmen named John and Alexander, whose identities are unknown. One of Annas's five sons was named Jonathan, and another was named Eleazer, so it's possible those were just other forms of these two men's names. Regardless, we do know that these men "were of high-priestly descent."

So Peter and John faced this array of men who'd done their best to discredit and dispose of Jesus.

b. Interaction with the Sanhedrin

The Sanhedrin usually assembled within the Temple grounds in the Hall of Hewn Stones, where they seated themselves in a semicircle with the president facing them. Prisoners were then "placed . . . in the center" (v. 7).

What an exciting moment—do you see what God did? He gave Peter and John the opportunity to preach to Israel's spiritually bankrupt leaders. This is a good example of how Satan cannot thwart God, and how persecution actually opens gospel avenues that otherwise wouldn't have existed. Peter and John's submission placed them in this unique position to carry their testimony to the Sanhedrin itself.

If you are obedient to God and get persecuted for righteousness' sake, accept the persecution as part of His perfect plan for you. God uses even Satan's fierce opposition for His glory and our good.

c. Interrogation by the Sanhedrin

"By what power, or in what name, have you done this?" (v. 7). God set the stage perfectly—the Jewish religious leaders' repeated demand, emphasizing the question of authority, perfectly prefaced Peter's preaching.

Note again how key the apostles' submission was to everything that God brought about. Peter says in 1 Peter 4, "Beloved, do not be surprised at the fiery ordeal among you, which comes upon you for your testing, as though some strange thing were happening to you"—the world won't be amenable to your faithfulness to Christ. Peter continues, "But to the degree that you share the sufferings of Christ, keep on rejoicing, so that also at the revelation of His glory you may rejoice with exultation. If you are reviled for the name of Christ, you are blessed, because the Spirit of glory and of God rests on you" (vv. 12–14). Verse 19 adds, "Therefore, those also who suffer according to the will of God shall entrust their souls to a faithful Creator in doing what is right." When you are persecuted, entrust yourself to God, that He may be glorified.

## B. Be Filled with the Holy Spirit (v. 8)

"Then Peter, filled with the Holy Spirit, said to them . . ."

The key to the Christian life is relying on the Holy Spirit's power. The phrase "filled with the Holy Spirit" is an aorist passive in Greek, which indicates that Peter was prepared for his situation because he was yielded to the Spirit's control.

### 1. The concept

The Spirit's filling does not come from agonizing over one's sins, going through some other emotional experience, or saying lengthy prayers. A believer is filled with the Spirit simply by walking in obedience to the Word and the Spirit (cf. Col. 3:16; Eph. 5:18–19). Peter was already Spirit filled because he was living obediently—he was preaching the gospel in submission even when the result was persecution.

The Holy Spirit indwells every Christian (John 14:17; cf. Rom. 8:9), empowering him. A Spirit-filled person yields to the Holy Spirit's power, which releases the expression of that power in the believer's life.

2. The conquest

The natural reaction in Peter's situation might have been to collapse under fear. And Peter knew he would have no victory in his circumstance unless he leaned his whole weight on the Spirit of God. He also knew that that was the guaranteed path to victory.

This is another way God uses persecution for good. Part of Peter's victory was that his persecution drew him closer to God and pushed him to live fully yielded to the Spirit's direction. That is true victory.

---

## CHRISTIAN COWARDICE

Christian victory is, in the face of adversity, to stand firm and yield to the Spirit, asking, "What is Your design? I submit to it." Much of the church today lacks victory because Christians are not leaning on the Spirit of God. We try to soften persecution by leaving out what's offensive about the gospel or talking in innocuous religious platitudes. Instead of boldly saying what is right and expectantly relying on God's Spirit for the results, we defeat ourselves by failing to speak the truth. Offense is a means God uses to show people their spiritual problem—

we shouldn't fear offending for the gospel's sake.

A Spirit-filled church will be uncomfortable in the world— but it will also be victorious. The church we see today is comfortable and defeated. When Peter and John found themselves out of step with the leaders of their day, they clashed with them in obedience to the Spirit who filled them. They necessarily collided with the spirit of the age— its selfishness, godlessness, immorality, and materialism. We fail in our Christian responsibilities when we fail to do the same.

---

### C. Be Bold and Use Opportunities to Preach (vv. 8–13)

"'Rulers and elders of the people, if we are on trial today for a benefit done to a sick man, as to how this man has been made well, let it be known to all of you and to all the people of Israel, that by the name of Jesus Christ the Nazarene, whom you crucified, whom God raised from the dead— by this name this man stands here before you in good health. He is the stone which was rejected by you, the builders, but which became the chief corner stone. And there is salvation in no one else; for there is no other name under heaven that has been given among men by which we must be saved.' Now as they observed the confidence of Peter and John and understood that they were uneducated and untrained men, they were amazed, and began to recognize them as having been with Jesus.'"

1. The confrontation with the Sanhedrin (vv. 8–10)

Peter, filled with the Spirit, used his persecution as an opportunity to testify boldly for Christ. Instead of being cowed or cautious, he said, "Let me tell you what I was preaching about so that you will understand it clearly." He then pointed out their opposition to God in crucifying Christ. Peter's message, just ninety-two Greek words, embodied all the characteristics of apostolic preaching: the sinner's indictment for rejecting Christ, Jesus' fulfillment of Messianic prophecy, His resurrection, and a closing invitation in verse 12 to believe.

Interestingly, Peter began his message by establishing the Sanhedrin's injustice to John and him—they were "on trial . . . for a benefit done to a sick man" whom they had "made well." Peter then hazards his life in verse 10, regardless of the council's now-seething anger. In the very citadel of the enemy, he proclaimed the resurrected Christ to those who had murdered Him. Doing so defied these religious leaders' claim to know God.

Peter boldly indicted Israel for executing Christ. He persisted in preaching about Christ's resurrection. Here is an important principle we can learn from Peter: Never accommodate the gospel by deleting things that offend others. You need to speak boldly even about the things that offend unbelievers.

## 2. The confirmation from Scripture (v. 11)

The Jewish leaders knew their own hypocrisy. They secretly may have feared that Christ really was the Messiah. Peter only compounded that by quoting from Psalm 118:22. Acts 4:11 reads, "[Jesus Christ] is the stone which was rejected by you, the builders, but which became the chief corner stone." Peter reminded the Sanhedrin that their own Scriptures prophesied that Messiah would be rejected and would rise again.

Construction in those days required a perfect cornerstone to square a building; an imperfect cornerstone would skew the whole structure. Some were immense—a temple cornerstone was found that measured thirty-eight feet long. Peter told the Sanhedrin that Psalm 118:22 had prophesied they would reject the cornerstone but that God would bring it back and establish it. God has made Christ the cornerstone on which His temple, the church, is built (Eph. 2:20). In Matthew 21:42, Jesus identified Himself as the cornerstone and also prophesied His rejection; Paul echoes those truths in Romans 9:33.

## 3. The call to the Savior (v. 12)

The popular claim is that there are many ways of salvation. In the city of Haifa in Israel, there is a Baha'i temple that has nine doors to God, each through a different religion. But Jesus said, "I am the way, and the truth, and the life; no one comes to the Father but through Me" (John 14:6). Peter closed with a powerful invitation to the Sanhedrin in Acts 4:12: "And there is salvation in no one else; for there is no other name under heaven that has been given among men by which we must be saved."

Christians are no narrower or stricter than the Word of God is. The Bible is never wrong—and it shows anything that contradicts it to be wrong. Scripture is strict about the way of salvation: A person can be saved only in Christ's name.

Peter plays on the Greek word he'd used of saving the lame man from his malady (v. 9) to tell the Sanhedrin that Christ is the only means by which they could be saved from their spiritual malady of sin and death.

---

## ALTARS OF COMPROMISE

In February of 1959, seventeen men on an expedition called Operation Deep Freeze IV went to the South Pole. In their spare time there, they built a sixteen-square-foot chapel they called "The Chapel of Our Faith." Inside it, they hung over an altar a picture of Jesus, a crucifix, a

Star of David, and a lotus leaf (representing Buddhism). An inscription on the wall read, "Now it can truly be said that the earth turns on a point of faith." Around 1970, a Midwestern university built an all-faiths, revolving altar whose four sides were dedicated, respectively, to Protestants, Catholics, Jews, and people of other faiths.

All of this may seem noble, except that Scripture is clear that there is no more than one way to God. Peter and John could easily have won the smiles of all and spared the early church vicious persecution by downgrading Jesus Christ and attempting to please their audience. Instead they chose to stand for what is true.

---

When you are persecuted, be submissive. Yield yourself to the Holy Spirit's control, and boldly use the opportunities that you have to preach the gospel. Those are the first three ways to be victorious over persecution.

## FOCUSING ON
## THE FACTS

1. How have Satan's techniques for persecuting the church changed over time? Why does he prefer making a Christian fall in love with the world even more than killing him?

2. What warning did Jesus give the church in John 15:18–20 and 16:2? How does 1 Peter 2:21 instruct us to live? When and why did unbelievers' response to the early church turn?

3. Describe the coalition of people involved in arresting Peter and John. Why did they oppose the apostles? How did Peter confront them in his message (vv. 9–12)?

4. How is persecution beneficial to the church? How does this reality help shape our attitude toward suffering persecution, and how did Peter and John exemplify that attitude? Connect 1 Peter 4 with your answer.

5. Explain how someone is filled with the Holy Spirit and what that means.

6. How did Peter confront the Sanhedrin in his message (Acts 4:10)? What important principle can we learn from Peter?

# PONDERING THE PRINCIPLES

1. If you fear being ridiculed when you talk about Christ, examine yourself and find out why. Who benefits from your fear, and what is the nature of that benefit? Who could benefit if you overcame it, and what is the nature of that benefit? Be honest: Which results are more important to you, and which are more important to God? Study and meditate on John 15:13; Matthew 7:13–14; Romans 10:13–14; and Mark 12:29–31.

2. Consider Scripture's testimony of those who lived filled with the Holy Spirit (e.g., Mic. 3:8; Luke 1:13–17; Acts 2:4). Remember Scripture's promise that you, as a believer, have the same Spirit indwelling you (cf. John 14:17; Rom. 8:9). Do you trust that God is in control of your circumstances even when you are actively persecuted? Consider a time you were persecuted for Christ in the past. How could you have relied more on the Spirit to make the most of that opportunity for the glory of God and the gospel?

3. While it is an increasingly offensive truth to hold, don't be afraid to tell an unbeliever that the only way he can be saved is through Christ (John 14:6; 1 Tim. 2:5). Memorize Acts 4:12 as a good verse to quote when sharing that truth with others: "There is salvation in no one else; for there is no other name under heaven that has been given among men by which we must be saved." Pray now for one person you know who needs this truth, and pursue an opportunity to speak it to them.

# HOW TO HANDLE
# PERSECUTION,
## PART 2

## INTRODUCTION

The book of Acts details for us the birth of the church and the beginning of its worldwide influence. In chapters 2 and 3, many came to Christ after hearing Peter's sermons. It is possible that by the time we come to chapter 4, there were twenty thousand people in the church. In Acts 4:4 alone, we read that five thousand men came to Christ, and many more women and children. The Jewish religious leaders felt very threatened by that. They had attempted to get rid of Jesus by executing Him, but now people were proclaiming that Christ rose from the dead. The Jewish leaders became scared, and they initiated religious and political opposition to the church. The rest of Acts documents the increasing severity of that persecution.

## A. The Fruit of Persecution

It's inevitable that if you live for Christ before the world, you'll provoke persecution because you're running contrary to Satan's system. But if handled biblically, persecution is a blessed experience, a positive rather than a negative.

### 1. Profiting from persecution

#### a. It brings maturity

James 1:2–4 says, "Consider it all joy, my brethren, when you encounter various trials, knowing that the testing of your faith produces endurance. And let endurance have its perfect result, so that you may be perfect and complete, lacking in nothing." Don't avoid persecution; through it, God will bring you to maturity. God accomplishes your perfection through two means: the Word of God (1 Pet. 2:2) and suffering. James 1:12 says, "Blessed is a man who perseveres under trial; for once he has been approved, he will receive the crown of life which the Lord has promised to those who love Him." Persecution brings maturity and reward.

# WHAT PERSECUTION IS NOT

Peter asks, "What credit is there if, when you sin and are harshly treated, you endure it with patience?" (1 Pet. 2:20). There is no glory in suffering the consequences of your own sins. "But if when you do what is right and suffer for it you patiently endure it, this finds favor with God. For you have been called for this purpose" (vv. 20–21). You were called to suffer.

But some people have misinterpreted that verse to mean that we must *make ourselves* suffer. Certain orders of the Roman Catholic Church encourage self-induced suffering. I once met a man of that group who wore a belt of sharp nails. He didn't understand suffering; he thought it was itself redemptive. There are "flagellants," who whip themselves with cords lined with glass shards until they bleed. They say they do so—and worse—in the name of Christ. They think they have to suffer—that their pain will merit God's favor and blessing. But their suffering comes from masochism, not from confronting the world with the gospel. Suffering that does not come from proclaiming Christ is not suffering *for* Christ.

God is only pleased by persecution that results from actively living a godly life in the world. That's what Peter was talking about in 1 Peter 2:20, and that's the persecution every Christian is called to suffer. Any other suffering cannot be considered persecution.

---

## b. It brings glory

First Peter describes the attitude we should have toward persecution: "To the degree that you share the sufferings of Christ, keep on rejoicing, so that also at the revelation of His glory you may rejoice with exultation. If you are reviled for the name of Christ, you are blessed, because the Spirit of glory and of God rests on you. But if anyone suffers as a Christian, he is not to be ashamed, but is to glorify God in this name" (4:13–14, 16). Glory is connected with persecution. First Peter 1:24 says, "All flesh is like grass, and all its glory like the flower of grass. The grass withers, and the flower falls off." Any earthly glory is temporary. Suffering for the gospel brings eternal glory and blessing—in addition to the growth and reward we already looked at.

First Peter 5:10 reads, "After you have suffered for a little while, the God of all grace, who called you to His eternal glory in Christ, will Himself perfect, confirm, strengthen and establish you." To be perfected, confirmed, strengthened, and established—to arrive where God wants you—you must endure suffering. Again, this is the suffering that results from confronting the world by proclaiming Jesus Christ with your life and your lips.

c. It brings victory

So the Christian can view persecution as wholly positive. Romans 8:35–37 says, "Who will separate us from the love of Christ? Will tribulation, or distress, or persecution, or famine, or nakedness, or peril, or sword? Just as it is written, 'For Your sake we are being put to death all day long; we were considered as sheep to be slaughtered.' But in all these things we overwhelmingly conquer through Him who loved us." We're expendable, yet we are conquerors. Victory is the growth, glory, joy, and reward that come through enduring persecution.

Paul testified to that in 2 Corinthians 12. Satan afflicted him with a thorn in the flesh, and God could have delivered him from it—Paul prayed for that. But the Lord answered, "My grace is sufficient for you, for power is perfected in weakness" (v. 9). Paul's reliance on the Lord was greater in his suffering. The apostle's response: "Therefore I am well content with weaknesses, with insults, with distresses, with persecutions, with difficulties, for Christ's sake; for when I am weak, then I am strong" (v. 10).

God save us from a placid life free of persecution. Suffering forces us to lean on Jesus—it shows us we can't make it on our own.

## 2. Persisting through persecution

### a. For others

Paul told the Philippians, "But even if I am being poured out as a drink offering upon the sacrifice and service of your faith, I rejoice and share my joy with you all" (Phil. 2:17). Paul could have thought, "I don't need to let myself be persecuted. I'm saved; I'm Spirit filled; I don't need to receive my joy from suffering." Instead, he derived joy from being offered up so that the Philippians might find *their* joy in Christ. Paul was undeterred even at being jailed for the gospel because he found blessing in persecution if it meant others might come to Christ. He wanted to spend his life for others.

Your life is expendable. Even if you die in the course of bringing someone to Christ, it is a blessing. If you have the opportunity to share about Christ with someone, but you don't in order to protect yourself, then you have prioritized your personal comfort

over another's salvation. Suffering is not
intrinsically joyful, but persecution is an
opportunity to suffer for someone else's sake.
You will understand the blessing of persecution
only when you can say with the apostle Paul,
"I will sacrifice myself for others."

b. For the Lord

Colossians 1:24 is a much-misunderstood
verse, but it gives the second reason that Paul
suffered, and it is a beautiful truth. "I, Paul,
was made a minister. Now I rejoice in my
sufferings for your sake" (vv. 23–24)—that
reiterates Paul's first reason for suffering. He
continues, "And in my flesh I do my share on
behalf of His body, which is the church, in
filling up what is lacking in Christ's afflictions"
(v. 24).

1) Explained

The world persecuted Jesus when He was
on earth, and it still hates Him today. It
persecutes you because you proclaim Him
(John 15:18). The persecuted Christian
is simply getting the hatred the world
directs at Christ because it can't reach Him
anymore.

Paul understood that reality. That's
what Colossians 1:24 is about, and so is
Galatians 6:17: "I bear on my body the

brand-marks of Jesus." Paul's attitude was to joyfully suffer for Christ after Christ had suffered so much for him.

## 2) Exemplified

We all have people we would willingly suffer for. If one of your children went through something extremely painful, you might think, "I would have gone through that for him." Perhaps you know someone who is in such anguish now, you wish you could bear it for him. We'd willingly substitute ourselves for those we love deeply. That's how Paul loved Jesus. The apostle readily endured persecution for Christ because it was necessary for the church's blessing—and even more fundamentally, because of his love for Christ and His glory.

## 3) Expected

Jesus warned, "You will be hated by all because of My name" (Mark 13:13). Paul testified, "The sufferings of Christ are ours in abundance" (2 Cor. 1:5), and, "[I am] always carrying about in the body the dying of Jesus" (4:10). He wrote to the Philippians, "That I may know Him and the power of His resurrection and the fellowship of His sufferings, being conformed to His death" (Phil. 3:10).

To Paul, persecution meant he was so representative of Christ that he kept getting what the world meant for Christ. That is part of how Paul could count it joy.

Persecution is good for God's people. It produces growth, gives us joy and blessing, and glorifies God. Persecution brings salvation and encouragement to those whom we reach. It allows us the privilege of identifying with Christ by bearing, in His place, the afflictions meant for Him. Many of us need to adjust our perspective on persecution.

## REVIEW

## I. THE PERSECUTION MANIFEST (ACTS 4:1–4)

## II. THE PERSECUTION MET (ACTS 4:3, 5–32)

### A. Be Submissive in Persecution (vv. 3, 5–7)

Peter and John did not resist their arrest. Even when they were before the Sanhedrin, they were cooperative with their captors. Peter and John weren't cowards. They were submissive, knowing that God was in control and that He would use them in a special way. Paul and Silas exhibited the same submissive attitude toward persecution that Peter and John show us here. When an earthquake gave Paul the opportunity to escape the Philippian jail, he didn't leave (Acts 16:25–28) because he knew God had a purpose for putting him there. And because he stayed, God used him to share Christ with the jailer and his family (vv. 29–34). Whenever God places you in a situation where you are persecuted, don't fight. Be submissive, and see what God is going to do.

**B. Be Filled with the Holy Spirit (v. 8)**

**C. Be Bold and Use Opportunities to Preach (vv. 8–13)**

1. The confrontation with the Sanhedrin (vv. 8–10)

2. The confirmation from the Scripture (v. 11)

3. The call to the Savior (v. 12)

## L E S S O N

4. The consequence of the sermon (v. 13)

Acts 4:13 says, "Now as they observed the confidence of Peter and John and understood that they were uneducated and untrained men, they were amazed." The Sanhedrin couldn't imagine two unlearned men handling a disputation with the Jewish Supreme Court and coming out on top. The two apostles also had such bold confidence in the face of possible death that it shocked the Sanhedrin.

The end of the verse says the council "began to recognize them as having been with Jesus." Like Jesus, the one who amazed the crowds by "teaching them as one having authority" (Matt. 7:28–29), Peter and John came out of nowhere and had done a miracle. Additionally, and again like Jesus, they handled the Old Testament masterfully. Peter and John followed in His footsteps under the Holy Spirit's inspiration.

So the Sanhedrin recognized that these men who had been with Jesus were resurrecting the same problems they'd had with Him. No one could equal Jesus in person, but Peter and John carried on His ministry in their miracles and message because He continued working through them.

## D. Be Obedient to God at All Costs (vv. 14–22)

### 1. The predicament (vv. 14–16)

#### a. Dumbfounded (v. 14)

"And seeing the man who had been healed standing with them, they had nothing to say in reply."

The Sanhedrin could say nothing to the apostles. The healed man stood before them, and by that time seems to have been standing on his own feet for three hours. That is a long time, considering that he had been crippled for forty years. Peter and John had performed a miracle. The Sanhedrin didn't know what to do. Notice that though they couldn't deny the miracle, they wouldn't accept it either. There they were, face-to-face with the truth and power of Christ, yet they were blinded by their own sin. John 3:19–20, "This is the judgment, that the Light has come into the world, and men loved the darkness rather than the Light." Why? "For their deeds were evil. For everyone who does evil hates the Light, and does not come to the Light for fear that his deeds will be exposed." The Sanhedrin knew the truth, but they avoided it.

Jesus told a group of Pharisees in John 8:44–45, "You are of your father the devil . . . . He is a liar and the father of lies. But because I speak the truth, you do not believe Me." He was saying that they found lies intelligible but could not understand the truth because of their evil nature.

## THE CHARACTER OF UNBELIEF

People frequently claim they'll believe if God does a

miracle for them. They may phrase it as a challenge: "If there is a God, why doesn't He do a miracle to prove His existence?"

Luke 16 tells a parable of two men who died: a beggar named Lazarus and a rich man. Lazarus went to "Abraham's bosom," and the rich man went to hell (vv. 22–23). The rich man cried to Abraham, "I beg you, father, that you send him to my father's house—for I have five brothers—in order that he may warn them, so that they will not also come to this place of torment" (vv. 27–28). Abraham replied, "If they do not listen to Moses and the Prophets, they will not be persuaded even if someone rises from the dead" (v. 31). That was true for many even at Christ's resurrection. Miracles don't bring people to belief in God; brokenness of spirit over the conviction of sin, accompanied by a knowledge of the truth does. Miracles had limited use even during Jesus' earthly life.

---

### b. Debating (vv. 15–16)

> "But when they had ordered them to leave the Council, they began to confer with one another, saying, 'What shall we do with these men? For the fact that a noteworthy miracle has taken place through them is apparent to all who live in Jerusalem, and we cannot deny it.'"

The Sanhedrin sent the healed man and the

apostles out while they privately debated
what to do. They were at a loss. They didn't
want to accept what Peter and John had
done. How terrible was the blackness of their
unbelief! Unable to deny the miracle, still
they were intent on rejecting it and ridding
themselves of the apostles. Their unbelief was
of the highest degree. The Sanhedrin needed
to have a secret meeting to decide what to do.
There were no laws against doing miracles or
good deeds. But they couldn't punish Peter
and John, now popular heroes, and risk
displeasing the crowds.

2. The prohibition (vv. 17–20)

a. The restraint upon the apostles (vv. 17–18)

"'But so that it will not spread any further
among the people, let us warn them to speak
no longer to any man in this name.' And when
they had summoned them, they commanded
them not to speak or teach at all in the name
of Jesus."

The Sanhedrin fell back on their authority.
Notice also, that the early church had to
be commanded to keep quiet—the modern
church has to be commanded to speak! Think
how different church history would have been
if Peter and John had obeyed the high court's
demand.

The Greek word for "speak" in verses 17 and 18 is unusual and appears only one other place in the New Testament. It means "to speak publicly." The Sanhedrin tried to ban preaching about Jesus, but Peter and John recognized a higher authority: Jesus had commanded them to preach the gospel to everyone (Mark 16:15).

b. The response of the apostles (vv. 19–20)

1) Expressed

If given that same command, most of us would have at least waited to exit the Sanhedrin's court before continuing to preach. Not Peter and John. They said, "Whether it is right in the sight of God to give heed to you rather than to God, you be the judge" (Acts 4:19). With holy courage, they denounced these leaders for opposing God and reminded them that He was the ultimate authority over them all.

2) Explained

Romans 13:1 says, "Every person is to be in subjection to the governing authorities. For . . . those which exist are established by God." Peter, too, affirmed that we are to be subject to all civil magistrates (1 Pet. 2:13–14). But recall Daniel's example: When his king decreed that all prayer could be only to the king himself, Daniel continued praying to God (Dan. 6:6–10). Christians should be the finest citizens possible, but when the command of men contradicts obedience to Christ, you must obey Christ.

Notice that Peter and John don't cause a scene. They simply say, "We cannot stop speaking about what we have seen and heard" (Acts 4:20). Peter and John realized they were in danger, but they saw their lives as expendable, and they wanted to be obedient at all costs. In Acts 5:29, when the apostles were arrested a second time, they said the same thing: "We must obey God rather than men." They didn't try to get out of their situation; they courageously stated who their authority was. It's been said the trouble with many Christians is that the voice of their neighbors is louder in their ears than the voice of God.

## 3) Exemplified

There were crucial times even in Israel's history when their obedience to God required disobedience to their government. In Exodus 1:16, Pharaoh commanded the midwives to kill every male Hebrew baby at birth. Verse 17 says, "But the midwives feared God, and did not do as the king of Egypt had commanded them, but let the boys live." So in verse 22, Pharaoh commanded, "Every son who is born you are to cast into the Nile, and every daughter you are to keep alive." But Moses's mother and sister also refused that edict (Ex. 2). God used all of those women to preserve the entire nation of Israel.

Whenever a conflict arises between a command of God and a command from men, we are to obey God. The apostles could not be silent about Christ. Likewise, Paul wrote, "Woe is me if I do not preach the gospel!" (1 Cor. 9:16, NKJV).

3. The pardon (vv. 21–22)

"When they [the Sanhedrin] had threatened them further, they let them go (finding no basis on which to punish them) on account of the people, because they were all glorifying God for what had happened; for the man was more than forty years old on whom this miracle of healing had been performed."

Concerned as the Sanhedrin was about its prestige and political position, and fearing the apostles' popularity with the people, the Jewish leaders could only threaten Peter and John and set them free. Peter and John were completely obedient to God's will, which protected them— even when persecution broke out, it did not break them.

Never stop obeying God just because of persecution. Don't let bribes, threats, mental persecution, or physical persecution take away your zeal. Never let anything make you violate the commands of our Lord Jesus Christ.

### E. Bind Yourselves Closer Together (v. 23)

"When they had been released, they went to their own companions . . ."

Persecution is an important ingredient for the unity of the body of Christ because it drives people together. We too readily make church life about who's wearing what or who said or did what to whom else—picayune concerns. If we were confronting the world with truth as we should be, we'd be too busy with the backlash for such silly matters, and we'd be more unified in the love and security of the body. As it is, we're not in enough trouble to think we need anyone else.

Acts 4:32 says that the early church was "of one heart and soul; and not one of them claimed that anything belonging to him was his own, but all things were common property to them." If anyone had a need, someone else met it (vv. 33–35).

### F. Bless the Lord (vv. 23–28)

1. Praising God's sovereignty

a. The acclaim for God's sovereignty (vv. 23–24)

"... and reported all that the chief priests and the elders had said to them. And when they heard this, they lifted their voices to God with one accord and said, 'O Lord, it is You who made the heaven and the earth and the sea, and all that is in them ...'"

Upon hearing Peter and John's report, the apostles' friends didn't cringe before the Sanhedrin's threats either—they praised God. They praised Him as the Creator and sovereign of all things. No one adopted the "better a live chicken than a dead lion" philosophy; Peter and John came back rejoicing that they were worthy to suffer for Jesus, and that their arrest provided the platform for them being filled with the Spirit and then preaching to the Sanhedrin. What could have been greater? The whole group of believers was like Joshua or Caleb—willing to risk their lives for their faith in God, out of obedience to His commands. Their reaction to persecution was to joyfully praise the Lord.

The Greek word for "Lord" in verse 24 is notable, as well. It gave us the English word *despot*, which refers to an absolute dictatorship. These believers recognized Christ's absolute lordship and praised God for exhibiting it in His creation.

b. The accomplishment of God's sovereignty (vv. 25–28)

They then quoted Psalm 2:1–2 in Acts 4:25–26, saying, "Who by the Holy Spirit, through the mouth of our father David Your servant, said, 'Why did the Gentiles rage, and the peoples devise futile things? The kings of the earth took their stand, and the rulers were gathered together against the Lord and against His Christ.'" In other words, "Lord, as far back as Psalm 2, You said that the world would oppose and kill Jesus. You know all about the persecution we are enduring too—You foretold it."

Verses 27–28 continue, "For truly in this city there were gathered together against Your holy servant Jesus, whom You anointed, both Herod and Pontius Pilate, along with the Gentiles and the peoples of Israel, to do whatever Your hand and Your purpose predestined to occur." Isn't that amazing? Even when Jesus' enemies murdered Him, they were accomplishing God's plan. Psalm 76:10 says God makes even the wrath of man to praise Him. All of Satan and the world's hatred could do nothing to interfere with the Lord's plan of salvation. These young believers likewise knew that the God who used Jesus' persecution to bring about salvation would certainly turn their persecution into something wonderful too. They trusted Him and rejoiced. Can you do the same in your own persecution?

## 2. Proclaiming God's sovereignty

I'm reminded of Joseph. First he was persecuted by his brothers, who hated him enough to kill him but sold him into slavery instead (Gen. 37:8, 27–28). Then Potiphar's wife made serious false accusations about him which landed him in prison (39:20). Then, though Joseph aided a fellow inmate, that man forgot about him (40:23). But God concluded all of this persecution by exalting Joseph (41:40–44), placing him so that he could directly help and sustain many, including those who had persecuted him. In Genesis 50:20, Joseph tells his brothers, "As for you, you meant evil against me, but God meant it for good in order to bring about this present result, to preserve many people alive."

God turns even evil into good. That is the perspective we should keep when persecuted, and it's the one that prompted the apostles and their companions to praise God in Acts 4:24–28.

## G. Beseech God for Greater Boldness (vv. 29–32)

## 1. The prayer (vv. 29–30)

"And now, Lord, take note of their threats, and grant that Your bond-servants may speak Your word with all confidence, while You extend Your hand to heal, and signs and wonders take place through the name of Your holy servant Jesus."

They immediately sought to return to the thick of it. They referred to themselves as the Lord's slaves and asked Him for "all boldness" (NKJV) to continue preaching the gospel. They were looking not for an out, but an in. Those Christians didn't seek to escape persecution or enemies; they asked for God's power to face them.

## 2. The power (vv. 31–32)

"And when they had prayed, the place where they had gathered together was shaken, and they were all filled with the Holy Spirit and began to speak the word of God with boldness" (v. 31). God powerfully demonstrated that He was answering their prayer. Persecution had an effect on the early church, but it was not the effect that Satan desired. "And the congregation of those who believed were of one heart and soul; and not one of them claimed that anything belonging to him was his own, but all things were common property to them" (v. 32). They went away from that prayer energized and preaching the gospel everywhere, and countless people came to salvation. They asked God for power, and He gave it.

Some of us have never experienced what the early church did because we've never lived godly or confronted the world. But that is the path of blessing in persecution. Some will crumble before it. But if you live godly—that is, submit in persecution, be filled with the Spirit by obeying Him at all costs, blessing the Lord and boldly taking opportunities to preach the gospel—then yours is the victory, the growth, the reward, and the joy.

## FOCUSING ON
## THE FACTS

1. It's counterintuitive to think of persecution as a conduit of blessing, but explain what the book of James tells us about how that can be the case. What happens to the one who endures persecution (Jas. 1:12; 1 Pet. 4:13–14, 16; 5:10)? Identify and explain the guardrails 1 Peter 2:20–21 gives us for thinking about the nature of persecution.

2. Why is the gospel worth suffering for? Cite some Scripture you're basing your answer and reasoning on. What do you demonstrate about your priorities if you seek to avoid that suffering? What does it say about your identity if you undertake gospel suffering?

3. How did the Sanhedrin respond to Peter and John generally? To the fact that they had healed the lame man? Why?

4. How did Peter and John respond to the Sanhedrin's command? How did their companions? Explain the principle of obedience that the apostles demonstrated. Why did their friends quote Psalm 2:1–2? What did they pray for? What did they not pray for?

## PONDERING THE PRINCIPLES

1. Persecution is an important ingredient for unity in the body of Christ. Find someone who is enduring persecution for Christ now, and support him in it. Share that person's suffering by praying with him, encouraging him in the truth, and praising God with him.

2. When you pray to God about the persecution you receive in Christ's name, what do you ask Him for? A way out of it? Strength to endure it? List what would happen if God granted you the first alternative. Consider the answers to the following questions in doing so: What would God's perspective be? What impact could you have in the world? What would happen to you? Now list what would happen if you sought the second alternative. Don't let persecution discourage you. Remember that as a foe of Satan, persecution will come. Commit yourself to God's care (1 Pet. 4:19; 5:7), and ask Him for boldness in the midst of persecution.

# THE PERSECUTED
# CHURCH
# REACHES OUT

## INTRODUCTION

Chapter 8 marks a transition in the book of Acts. It records the second phase of the church's missionary outreach, as it took the gospel message from Jerusalem out to the farther regions of Judea and Samaria. The catalyst for that transition was the martyrdom of Stephen.

### A. The Question Surrounding Stephen's Martyrdom

#### 1. Asked

A missionary told an American audience about a fellow missionary who had attempted to rescue a Muslim Arab boy who was drowning in the ocean. That colleague dashed into the surf, and somehow, the little boy survived—but the missionary drowned. After the speaker finished, someone asked him, "Isn't it pointless for a well-trained, strategic individual like that missionary to give his life for a Muslim Arab boy?"

We could be tempted to ask the same type of question, regarding Stephen. He had many capabilities—he was dynamic, Spirit filled, and emulated Christ in handling the Old Testament well. Why should such a man have such a brief ministry? Wasn't it a waste for him to embroil himself in a situation that would cost him his life?

His speech to the Sanhedrin in Acts 7 seemed to yield nothing but an aggressively negative response, as seen in his immediate murder. That event then triggered the persecution of all Christians. Stephen's testimony enraged a Jew named Saul, who set about killing Christians and trying to extinguish the church. A cursory view could make Stephen's death look like mere tragedy—both personally for him and corporately, in fracturing the new church's fragile fellowship. But that kind of thinking fails to understand how the Holy Spirit works.

## 2. Answered

The Holy Spirit is in the business of turning disasters into blessings, and tragedies into victories. Throughout Acts, we see the Holy Spirit turn every instance of persecution into a powerful opportunity for preaching the gospel, especially in areas that otherwise would not have been reached. Like trying to stamp out a fire, the more forcefully the persecutors tried to extinguish the church, the more they scattered its embers to start blazes in new places. God uses persecution to accomplish His work.

## B. The Catalyst That Spread the Kingdom

### 1. What persecution did to the church

#### a. The people dispersed

The church's first great missionary movement began through persecution. The church was based in Jerusalem, and persecution spread it to Judea and Samaria. Tertullian said, "The blood of the martyrs is the seed of the church" (*Apologeticus*, 50, 13). Stephen's death was a catalyst for the spread of the gospel message. In fact, persecution was so much a part of preaching Christ that the Greek word for *witness* was *martur*, from which we get *martyr*. So Acts 8 shows Stephen's martyrdom catalyzing believers' spread to Samaria, Judea, Antioch, Cyprus, Asia Minor, and finally Europe.

### b. The pattern demonstrated

The church began with a strong Jewish flavor. In Acts 6, we see the first step of its expansion beyond the Jerusalem Jews as Stephen began to preach to Hellenistic Jews—that is, those who lived in mainstream Greek culture. The Greek names of the men selected to serve the church (Acts 6:5) show that those Jews were also coming to Christ. But in Acts 8, the church extends into the Gentile world; by the end of that chapter, Philip is well outside of Jewish spheres.

That fulfilled the pattern Jesus gave for the church's expansion: "You will receive power when the Holy Spirit has come upon you; and you shall be My witnesses both in Jerusalem, and in all Judea and Samaria, and even to the remotest part of the earth" (Acts 1:8). That outlines the book of Acts: The church begins in Jerusalem, then spreads to Judea and Samaria, then to the rest of the world. The Samaritans, being part Jewish and part Gentile, formed a bridge to the Gentile world.

## 2. What persecution did to Jerusalem

While it is exciting to see the gospel message spreading in Acts 8, it's also sad to see the door begin to shut on Jerusalem. Though it was dominant in the first seven chapters of Acts, it fades into the background for the rest of the book and reminds us that an opportunity ignored is an opportunity lost. Jesus said that "salvation is from the Jews" (John 4:22); Paul said of the gospel, "It is the power of God for salvation to everyone who believes, *to the Jew first* and also to the Greek" (Rom. 1:16, emphasis added). God extended the saving gospel to Israel first. But as they always had, the Jewish people rejected the truth. Their leaders demonstrated the depth of their antagonism to Christianity by killing Stephen. But even this tragedy for Israel is a blessing for the Gentiles.

# LESSON

The church expanded progressively, through persecution, which led to the wider preaching of the gospel and yielded the produce of transformed lives.

## I. THE PERSECUTION (ACTS 8:1–3)

Up to Acts 8, persecution of the church had been sporadic—Peter and John had been jailed more than once. But Stephen's murder sparked widespread persecution of Christians. The central figure in that campaign was a man named Saul from the tribe of Benjamin (Phil. 3:5), likely named after King Saul.

## A. Saul's Debut (vv. 1–2)

### 1. The postscript about Stephen's death (v. 1)

"Saul was in hearty agreement with putting him to death. . . ."

#### a. The support

Acts 8:1 really starts with a postscript to Stephen's stoning in Acts 7: "Saul was in hearty agreement with putting him to death." Acts 7:58 tells us that Stephen's murderers avidly set about their work, "[laying] aside their robes at the feet of a young man named Saul." Saul was from Cilicia (22:3), so it is very likely he had argued with Stephen in the synagogue of Hellenistic Jews there (6:9). Saul was brilliant. He was a Pharisee, zealous for Judaism, and deeply committed to all he undertook. He was zealous in killing Christians, but God redirected that zeal at Saul's conversion, which is cause for great praise.

Saul likely fomented Stephen's martyrdom, involved as he probably had been in the conflict with Stephen from early on. Little did Saul know that one day he would endure far more for Christ than Stephen did. Stephen was blessed to die immediately; Paul endured intense assault again and again before he was finally beheaded in Rome. In Acts 9, God testified, "I will show [Paul] how much he must suffer for My name's sake" (v. 16).

## b. The similarity

It's interesting, as you study Paul, how many parallels his life had with Stephen's. Both men had their testimonies rejected, were disputed against in synagogues, and were accused of blasphemy. Stephen was accused of speaking against Moses, the law, and the Temple (Acts 6:11, 13). Paul was accused of speaking against one or more of the same at least four different times (21:28; 24:6; 25:8; 28:17). Stephen was dragged out of a city (7:58), and so was Paul (14:19). Both were brought before the Sanhedrin; both were stoned. They were both martyred for Christ.

All that Paul gloated about on the day of Stephen's murder, he himself later suffered to greater degree for the cause of Christ. Yet in Christ, Paul saw it all not as punishment but as glory—that's a serious change in attitude.

## c. The savagery

### 1) Toward Stephen

The Greek word for "death" in Acts 8:1 is vivid. Ancient Greek writings used it often as a medical term to indicate destruction. The use of that word indicates that

Stephen died horribly—not mere death but destruction, under the stones they hurled at him.

2) Toward the church

Stephen's stoning seems to have set off the Jews, as if they were piranhas who grew more frenzied by the first bloodshed. This began the fulfillment of the Lord's words in John 15:18–19, "If the world hates you, you know that it has hated Me before it hated you. . . . Because you are not of the world, but I chose you out of the world, because of this the world hates you." Jesus also told His disciples, "They will make you outcasts from the synagogue, but an hour is coming for everyone who kills you to think that he is offering service to God" (16:2). So the enemies of the church sought to shred it, and Saul was their prime architect and mover.

2. The pursuit after Stephen's death (v. 1)

". . . And on that day a great persecution began against the church in Jerusalem, and they were all scattered throughout the regions of Judea and Samaria, except the apostles."

We don't have the specifics of Saul's offensive, but whatever he did, it drove Christians out of Jerusalem and scattered them abroad. The group of Christians who experienced that the worst may have been the Hellenistic Jews, due to association with Stephen. Most of the believers who remained were former Jews originally from Jerusalem; perhaps some of them simply couldn't flee.

So "they were all scattered abroad . . . except the apostles" (KJV). The courageous apostles stayed in Jerusalem. They stayed at their posts to nurture the believers who remained and to continue evangelizing the lost. The Jewish leaders had rejected Christ, but the people were still coming to Him, as verse 2 shows.

3. The protest over Stephen's death (v. 2)

"Some devout men buried Stephen, and made loud lamentation over him."

"Devout men" remained in Jerusalem. I don't think that refers to Christians; they would have been called "believers" or "brothers." "Devout men" likely denotes pious Jews (cf. Luke 2:25; Acts 2:5), perhaps friends of Stephen from the synagogue he'd attended. So there was still some fertile soil for the gospel in Jerusalem.

Jewish law required appropriate burial for criminals but also forbid lamentation over their death. But these devout men not only buried Stephen, they wept over him in public protest of his murder. It was for people like them that the apostles remained in Jerusalem.

James later led the church in Jerusalem, and it remained the center of the early church's development—recall Acts 15 and the meeting of the great Jerusalem Council. But a huge number of the first Christians fled Jerusalem early on.

## B. Saul's Deeds (v. 3)

"But Saul began ravaging the church, entering house after house, and dragging off men and women, he would put them in prison."

### 1. The energy behind the persecution

Saul didn't hold back. He went right down the block and delivered any Christian he found to prison. And he did so with the full authority of the Jewish leaders; in Acts 26:9–11, Paul said, "[I did] many things hostile to the name of Jesus of Nazareth. And this is just what I did in Jerusalem; not only did I lock up many of the saints in prisons, having received authority from the chief priests, but also when they were being put to death I cast my vote against them. And as I punished them often in all the synagogues, I tried to force them to blaspheme [i.e., renounce their faith]; and being furiously enraged at them, I kept pursuing them even to foreign cities."

### 2. The error behind the persecution

a. Saul's perspective

Saul thought he was doing right, and he really believed in what he was doing. In Galatians 1:13–14, he said, "You have heard of my former manner of life in Judaism, how I used to persecute the church of God beyond measure and tried to destroy it; and I was advancing in Judaism beyond many of my contemporaries among my countrymen, being more extremely zealous for my ancestral traditions." He thought he was pleasing God through his extreme zeal for Judaism, yet he was wrong.

Some say, "It doesn't matter what you believe, as long as you believe in something," or, "Look, they're religious; leave them alone." But perhaps no one believed more fervently than Paul, and that didn't stop him from being absolutely wrong. There is only one way to God, and that is through Jesus Christ (John 14:6).

b. Saul's penitence

Acts 8:3 says that Saul "began ravaging" the church. That wording indicates brutal and sadistic cruelty; in Greek literature it was used of a wild boar ravaging a vineyard or an animal savagely tearing apart prey.

This period really grieved Paul in years to come. All of us have sins we can't forget—

dumb, painful, hurtful, or foolish things. But imagine living with the knowledge that you slaughtered hundreds of fellow Christians. Paul testified of this in Acts 26, Galatians 1, and also in Acts 22:3–4: "I am a Jew, born in Tarsus of Cilicia, but brought up in this city, educated under Gamaliel, strictly according to the law of our fathers, being zealous for God just as you all are today. I persecuted this Way to the death, binding and putting both men and women into prisons." In verses 19–20, he adds, "Lord, they themselves understand that in one synagogue after another I used to imprison and beat those who believed in You. And when the blood of Your witness Stephen was being shed, I also was standing by approving, and watching out for the coats of those who were slaying him." It was hard for Paul to remember his days of raging against the church like a wild beast.

3. The extent of the persecution

Luke mentions in Acts 8:3 that Saul put both "men *and* women" (emphasis added) into prisons. Saul made no exceptions. Hebrews 10:32 speaks of the "great conflict of sufferings" that Christians endured, including the seizure of their possessions. It's possible that some who experienced the persecution at Jerusalem were later in the congregation that the book of

Hebrews was written to.

Acts 8:3 implies that Christians were deprived of all they owned. Notice the word "dragging"; it could also be translated "hauling" and is used in John 21:8 in the context of dragging a net full of fish from the ocean onto the shore. That was how Paul treated Christians.

## II. THE PREACHING (ACTS 8:4–7)

### A. Expanded (v. 4)

"Therefore, those who had been scattered went about preaching the word."

Don't gloss over the "therefore." Though they were being assailed and flung from their homes, these early Christians didn't simply hunker down to wait out the abuse; they picked up evangelizing wherever God had scattered them to—it was such a part of how they lived.

"Went about" translates a word used frequently in Acts of missionary efforts. What a beautiful spiritual reality. Picture them surging from the gates of Jerusalem to spread the gospel in the world. Every one of them was a preacher.

### B. Commanded (v. 4)

Some time ago, I was talking with a student who was working for a campus Christian organization. He said, "I think I've figured out why this ministry is so difficult for me—I don't have the gift of evangelism." I answered, "Evangelism is not a gift; it's a command." Jesus said in Mark 16:15, "Go into all the world and preach the gospel to all creation." He told the apostles, "You shall be My witnesses" (Acts 1:8). We are all commanded to evangelize.

---

# REFLECTING ON PERSECUTION

Several points from this passage really speak to my heart. First, that persecution tends to promote the very thing that it intends to destroy. Even Satan's best effort to wipe out the church through Saul simply played into God's plan to disperse His message. Also persecution is good for Christians because it turns them loose with zeal for new opportunities. Related to that, it tends to pare off the excess, get rid of the nonessentials. And these texts point out that no Christian can say, "That's not my job," regarding evangelism; every Christian should desire to share the gospel. That privilege belongs not just to a few but to all. Imagine if we all surged from the doors of our churches to bring the good news everywhere we went. You should be talking about Christ so much that no matter where God has you, you are evangelizing.

---

## C. Exemplified (vv. 5–7)

### 1. The missionary (v. 5)

To demonstrate what and how these first missionaries preached, the Holy Spirit selected one man as our example: Philip. He was one of seven men chosen to care for the Jerusalem church's business (Acts 6:5). He was a wonderful, Spirit-filled man, a prophet who, unusually, had four daughters who also prophesied (21:9). He is the only person that Scripture ever calls an evangelist (v. 8).

Ephesians 4:11 lists the different categories of gifted men God gave to the church: apostles, prophets, evangelists, and teaching pastors. By the end of the early church age, the founding apostles and prophets (cf. Eph. 2:20) were replaced by evangelists and teaching pastors as the church's key leaders. Evangelists reach out, win people to Christ, and establish churches. Teaching pastors stay with a church and instruct the people in its fellowship. But there was overlap in the transition of those offices—apostles and prophets to evangelists and pastors—which we see in Philip; he was the last of the prophets and the first of the evangelists.

2. The mission field (v. 5)

a. The place

> In Acts 8:5, we read, "Philip went down to the city of Samaria and began proclaiming Christ to them." Since Samaria is north of Jerusalem, people can be confused to read that "Philip went down" to get there. But Jerusalem is on a high plateau, so anyone leaving the city must go down to his destination.

> Samaria was the name of a region as well as the name of the city that had been its ancient capital when that area was the Northern Kingdom of Israel. Recall that the Jews were to have no dealings with the Samaritans, as the woman at the well evidenced when Jesus spoke to her (cf. John 4:9). But Philip acted strategically in going to Samaria.

---

## "HE WHO IS FAITHFUL IN A VERY LITTLE THING..."

Philip reminds us of the principle from Luke 16:10, "He who is faithful in a very little thing is faithful also in much" (cf. Matt. 25:21). Philip had been elected to particular service in the church because he exhibited the characteristics of faithful devotion to God (Acts

6:5). After that, God sent him to Samaria and greater responsibility.

People often approach me expressing their intention to go into ministry. I always tell them the same thing: that it's usually those who are faithful in what God has already given them to whom He then gives greater responsibility. So be faithful as a deacon, an evangelist, a Sunday school teacher, an elder, a pastor-teacher—whatever God has already given you to do, prove yourself faithful in it. The head of Wycliffe Bible Translators once told me they'd found that a person who is not an effective evangelist at home will be no more an effective evangelist on the mission field. I agreed; relocating your feet won't automatically change what's in your heart.

---

### b. The people

It wasn't easy for Philip to go to Samaria; Jews generally hated Samaritans. Following Solomon's death, Israel split into the Northern Kingdom (ten tribes ruled by Jeroboam) and the Southern Kingdom of Judah (the tribes of Judah and Benjamin, ruled by Rehoboam). In the eighth century BC, the Assyrians took the Northern Kingdom captive, leaving few Jews behind and moving other peoples into the land. The Jewish remnant, in unfaithfulness, intermarried with those foreigners and brought forth the Samaritans.

About five centuries before Christ's birth, the
Southern Kingdom returned from its own
seventy-year captivity to the Babylonians
when Cyrus of Persia overthrew Babylon
and decreed that Israel could return to its
land (Ezra 1:1–4). Ezra and Nehemiah led
the exiles back and began rebuilding the
Temple and the walls of Jerusalem. The
Samaritans from the north offered to help but
were contemptuously rebuffed (4:1–3); the
returning Jews wanted nothing to do with the
Samaritans because they had desecrated their
covenant with God by uniting with Gentiles.
That began the hatred between the Jews and
the Samaritans. We see it in the book of Acts—
and sometimes even still today.

So Philip, in obedience to the Holy Spirit and
in His energy, courageously undertook his
preaching mission.

3. The method (v. 5)

The word Acts 8:5 uses for Philip's ministry,
*kērussō*, is distinct from the description of
"preaching" in verse 4 (Gk., *euangelizō*). This
is the difference between "proclaiming" the
gospel as a public herald or preacher, and more
individual evangelism. Philip publicly proclaimed
Christ to the Samaritans.

4. The message (v. 5)

> "Christ" is the Greek equivalent of the Hebrew word *Messiah*. The Samaritans had retained certain aspects of Jewish belief, including belief in God and hope in the coming Messiah, as Jesus' encounter with the Samaritan woman in John 4 shows. Philip went to Samaria to present the simple message that Jesus Christ is the Messiah.

---

## MODERN MISSIONS

God had uniquely prepared the Samaritans to receive Philip's message by giving them the necessary context to understand it. Unlike the Samaritans, or many Jews still today, most Gentiles you encounter will not understand the importance of the statement, "Jesus Christ is the Messiah." Some people are more prepared than others to receive Christ, so be ready to explain the basics of who God is, what sin is, and what God's plan for the ages is. Give them the simple gospel, and be ready to answer their objections and questions. But most of all, remember that it is God who prepares the soil of men's hearts to receive the gospel, and that you must be ready to introduce them to Christ wherever or however you encounter them.

---

5. The answer (v. 6)

"The crowds with one accord were giving attention to what was said by Philip, as they heard . . ."
Miraculously, scores of Samaritans were spiritually awakened.

6. The authentication (vv. 6–7)

". . . and saw the signs which he was performing. For in the case of many who had unclean spirits, they were coming out of them shouting with a loud voice; and many who had been paralyzed and lame were healed."

God granted other miracles alongside Philip's preaching, as confirmation that Philip's message was from God.

a. Healing of spiritual ills

The Bible frequently talks about people who are possessed by unclean spirits, or demons. It calls them demoniacs or demonized, from *daimonizomai*.

1) The power of demons

We can tend to relegate demonic activity and possession to superstition and witchcraft, but demoniacs inhabit our own society—and probably more than you think. The possessed may not roll on the ground foaming at the mouth today. Satan is not stupid. He adapts his activity to the surrounding culture. We have suave, well-dressed, articulate, educated demoniacs in our society—some propagating their ideas in institutions of higher learning. They maintain enough apparent equilibrium to be heard and admired by the unwitting. So the demoniac's condition can run the gamut—sometimes demons cause bizarre and alarming behavior, but their activity more often is very subtle, especially in our society.

2) The power over demons

Jesus cast demons out with a word (Matt. 8:16); the apostles and others to whom He gave the gift of miracles could do the same. But the gift of miracles is not present in the church today; it belonged to the early church. Those who attempt it get frustrated when they find they can't. We have to pray for sick or demon-possessed people (Jas. 5:14–15). We can also help demoniacs by confronting them with their need for confession and cleansing so that the indwelling Holy Spirit makes it impossible for demons to occupy them again.

b. Healing of physical ills

The end of verse 7 says that Philip also healed
people suffering significant physical maladies.

## III. THE PRODUCT (ACTS 8:8–9)

"So there was much rejoicing in that city. Now there
was a man named Simon . . ."

Philip's preaching and miracles yielded a great response
from the people. People who receive preaching break
down into two categories: faithful and phony. Some
people truly become saved, and others may appear to
but don't. Simon was one of the phonies (vv. 9–24).
The two reactions to the gospel are represented in the
parable of the wheat and the tares (Matt. 13:24–30)
and the parable of the sower (Matt. 13:5–8). May
preaching in your life bring about true faith.

# FOCUSING ON
# THE FACTS

1. What kind of transition marks the beginning of Acts chapter 8? What catalyzed it? Connect that with how the Holy Spirit often chooses to work, and with the pattern we see established for the rest of the book of Acts. Explain Jerusalem's changing role in it all.

2. Who became the central figure leading persecution of the church? Why did the apostles remain in Jerusalem despite the savage persecution (cf. Acts 8:2)?

3. Characterize Saul's campaign of persecution from Scripture's description. How does this portion of his life illustrate how religious zeal alone is insufficient to please God? How is that affirmed in Paul's reflection on this period in later years?

4. Comment on the importance of the word "therefore" in Acts 8:4. Tie that to the church's ongoing responsibility as laid out in Mark 16:15 and Acts 1:8.

5. Explain why Acts 8 tells us so much about Philip and his ministry specifically—what pivotal transition did he embody in the church's development? Where did he go to preach, and why was that an unusual move?

6. What are the two ways people receive preaching? Examine Matthew 13:5–8 and 24–30; what do those parables tell us about true versus false faith?

## PONDERING THE PRINCIPLES

1. The Jewish religious leaders killed Stephen because of his strong stand for Christ. Read about Stephen in Acts chapters 6 and 7. In chapter 6, what do verses 5, 8, and 10 say about Stephen? What did Stephen talk to the Sanhedrin about in Acts 7:1–53? How did Stephen conclude his speech (vv. 51–53)? What was the Sanhedrin's reaction (vv. 54, 57–59)? What did Stephen say in verses 55–56, 60? Based on what you have just read, what qualities did Stephen have that we all should have when we witness for Christ?

2. As widespread persecution of Christians began and grew after Stephen's murder, it would have been easy to think that the early church couldn't last. But rather than destroying it, persecution strengthened and spread the church. The early Christians took advantage of their dispersion to preach the gospel in new places. Think of two or three specific instances when you have been persecuted for the gospel, and ask yourself regarding each: Did you respond the same way the first Christians did to their persecution? How did God use your situation for His purposes? (If you are not sure, how *could* God have used it?) Especially when you are experiencing persecution, remember that God is sovereign (Ps. 115:3; 1 Chron. 29:11), and that nothing happens outside His will. From now on, examine closely the persecution you endure, and think how God might be using it to accomplish His work.

3. Acts 8:4 tells us that the Christians who fled
   persecution in Jerusalem continued to preach
   wherever they went. Read Acts 14:5–7 and 1
   Thessalonians 2:2—did persecution silence Paul? Read
   Acts 20:22–24—what awaited Paul in Jerusalem, and
   why was he unafraid of that fate? Few of us are likely
   to be persecuted as Paul was, yet we are quick to shut
   our mouths when opposition comes our way. Read
   and meditate on 2 Corinthians 4:8–18. What was
   Paul's response to persecution, and why was he willing
   to endure it? Ephesians 3:20 says that God's power
   resides within all Christians. Are you living in harmony
   with the Holy Spirit, or are you sinfully resisting Him?
   Commit yourself to trusting and obeying the Lord by
   living for Him in the world, particularly by preaching
   His gospel of salvation (Mark 16:15).

# HOW TO TURN
# PERSECUTION
# INTO PRODUCTION

## INTRODUCTION

Acts 16 is a memorable chapter. It records unforgettable moments like Lydia's salvation (vv. 14–15), Paul and Silas's encounter with a demon-possessed woman (vv. 16–24), and then how God saved the Philippian jailer through an earthquake (vv. 25–40). That last narrative is the focus of this lesson. One particular facet of it leaps off the page because it poses the most important question a person could ever ask: "What must I do to be saved?" Paul and Silas gave the only true answer: "Believe in the Lord Jesus" (v. 31). There is only one way to be saved, and that is by believing in the Lord Jesus Christ. "There is salvation in no one else; for there is no other name under heaven that has been given among men by which we must be saved" (Acts 4:12). That is the story of salvation.

## A. The Plea

We tend to think that in presenting Christ to someone, we intrude upon his life. But people are looking for deliverance. Universally, man's heart seeks to answer the question, "What is life all about?" Don't shrink from helping him. The person in deep distress is ready to hear the message of salvation.

One indicator of man's desire to answer that ultimate question is the sheer number of religious systems people have invented. People want deliverance from meaninglessness, sin, guilt, boredom, loneliness, insecurity, anxiety, and the dread of death—so they look to a variety of panaceas.

## B. The Problem

### 1. Amplified by superficiality

The Philippian jailer was probably a hardened former Roman soldier. In those days, jails were dark, unsanitary, miserable places. Still, the jailer may have derived his sense of honor from the fact that Rome likely commissioned him to that post. Apart from Christ, every man eventually reduces his life to something to give it meaning. It can be money, prestige, popularity, or promotion.

Some people find meaning in life from a new car. When life gets dull again, they buy another car. Some people live only for sex, or for athletics, or for drink or drugs. But for some, when those repositories of meaning fall apart, they do too— they kill themselves.

In Acts 16:26, the jail fell apart. A great earthquake opened all of the prison doors and loosed all of the inmates' bonds. The jailer decided to kill himself (v. 27)—he knew that if all of his prisoners escaped, his own life would be forfeit.

2. Answered by salvation

But God had something else in mind for this man. And it involved Paul and Silas telling him, "Believe in the Lord Jesus, and you will be saved, you and your household" (v. 31). That's the main message of Acts 16:19–40—and the main message of Christianity.

## C. The Prologue

Let's look at what led up to our passage, to set the scene. Paul, Silas, Luke, and Timothy were all traveling together as a missionary team—probably the best that ever deployed.

1. Winning a soul

Their arrival at Philippi brought the gospel to Europe. On the Sabbath, God directed them to go "to a riverside, where [they] were supposing that there would be a place of prayer" (v. 13). There they met some women worshiping God who were either Jewish by birth or by proselytization. It seems there were not enough Jewish men in Philippi to found a synagogue, so the women gathered only at a little proseuche, an ancient name for a place of prayer. God sent His preachers to those women, and particularly to one named Lydia. "The Lord opened her heart" such that she and her whole household became saved (vv. 14–15). That was the beginning of the church in Europe.

2. Warring against Satan

Satan immediately launched his counterattack. The missionary team promptly met another woman in Philippi—a demon-possessed girl who followed them around, crying, "These men are bond-servants of the Most High God, who are proclaiming to you the way of salvation" (v. 17). Now why would that be Satan's message through his servant? Satan will agree with God long enough to gain people's trust—then he turns to his true evil purpose.

Paul knew this. He addressed not the girl but the evil spirit controlling her: "'I command you in the name of Jesus Christ to come out of her!' And it came out at that very moment" (v. 18).

The backlash to their freeing the enslaved girl set up what transpired in verses 19–40. Verse 19, "But when her masters saw that their hope of profit was gone, they seized Paul and Silas and dragged them into the market place before the authorities." Satan's plan to infiltrate the church failed, so he attempted another tack: persecution. Infiltration is Satan's most effective attack on the church. Infiltration works; persecution doesn't— the persecuted church simply grows. Still, Satan can't resist attacking believers by whatever means.

## D. The Precious Principle

A principle we see illustrated over and over in the book of Acts is that persecution results in blessings and growth. Persecution of the church in chapters 4 and 5 made it multiply; likewise even when persecution spread and intensified in chapter 8.

Persecution brings blessing; infiltration destroys the church. In fact, Satan is probably more active in the church today than at its start because we are *not* being persecuted. His present work is subtle and effective infiltration.

God overcame Satan's attempt to infiltrate the church through the demon-possessed girl in Acts 16:16–18. We now turn to the rest of the chapter to see how He overcame Satan's persecution of the church. Along the way we'll answer questions, including, How does God make a persecuted man productive? What is His process for bringing a positive result from a negative situation?

## LESSON

### I. SUFFERING PERSECUTION (ACTS 16:19–24)

#### A. The Provocation (v. 19)

Paul cast the demon out of the girl (v. 18). She had been "bringing her masters much profit by fortune-telling" (v. 16), but they likely gave her only a small portion of the money she earned. Their reaction in verse 19 shows that they obviously didn't care about the girl. They didn't rejoice in her supernatural deliverance; they thought only of their lost income.

1. The precedent

It's possible that that same focus was part of why the townspeople begged Jesus to leave after He cast the legion of demons from the Gadarene madman into the herd of swine (Mark 5:1–17). The people feared Jesus' power, but they may also have feared further financial losses.

2. The principle

Scripture explicitly warns that money can interfere with spiritual perception. "The love of money is a root of all sorts of evil, and some by longing for it have wandered away from the faith and pierced themselves with many griefs" (1 Tim. 6:10). Verse 9 of the same chapter says, "Those who want to get rich fall into temptation and a snare and many foolish and harmful desires which plunge men into ruin and destruction." It is not the having but rather the loving of money that is the problem. After the rich young ruler chose his earthly wealth over Christ, Jesus said, "How hard it will be for those who are wealthy to enter the kingdom of God!" (Mark 10:23). The disciples, astonished, asked, "Then who can be saved?" (v. 26). "Jesus said, 'With people it is impossible, but . . . all things are possible with God'" (v. 27).

3. The parallel

Later, Paul had been teaching day and night in Ephesus for three years (Acts 20:31), and many people were delivered from illness and demons, and many were becoming saved. Acts 19:18–20 says that "many also of those who had believed kept coming, confessing and disclosing their practices. And many of those who practiced magic brought their books together and began burning them in the sight of everyone; and they counted up the price of them and found it fifty thousand pieces of silver. So the word of the Lord was growing mightily and prevailing." The Word of God came to dominate the city of Ephesus.

"About that time there occurred no small disturbance concerning the Way. For a man named Demetrius . . . who made silver shrines of Artemis, was bringing no little business to the craftsmen; these he gathered together with the workmen of similar trades, and said, 'Men, you know that our prosperity depends upon this business. You see and hear that not only in Ephesus, but in almost all of Asia, this Paul has persuaded and turned away a considerable number of people, saying that gods made with hands are no gods at all. Not only is there danger that this trade of ours fall into disrepute, but also that the temple of the great goddess Artemis be regarded as worthless and that she whom all of Asia and the world worship will even be dethroned from her magnificence.' When they heard this and were filled with rage, they began crying out, saying, 'Great is Artemis of the Ephesians!' The city was filled with the confusion" (vv. 23–29).

Paul's preaching of the gospel ruined business for craftsmen in the idol trade. Likewise for the demon-possessed girl and her masters in Acts 16.

## B. The Praetors (vv. 19–20)

Her masters "seized Paul and Silas and dragged them into the market place before the authorities" (v. 19). What a role-reversal for Paul, who used to drag Christians out of their houses and off to prison (8:3). Remember what God told Ananias in Acts 9:15–16: that Paul was "a chosen instrument of Mine, to bear My name before the Gentiles and kings and the sons of Israel; for I will show him how much he must suffer for My name's sake." It's likely Paul was recalling those moments while he was himself dragged away—but we know Paul well enough to know he must also have seen this as an opportunity for Christ.

"Market place" in Greek is *agora*, equivalent to the Latin *forum*. Paul and Silas were dragged to the city center, where the senate houses, courts, temples, and public offices were. The "chief magistrates" (v. 20) and dignitaries of the city congregated there. Every Roman colony in a Greek city had two magistrates—two praetors—invested with supreme authority in that city.

## C. The Prejudice (v. 20)

The girl's masters expressed anti-Semitic contempt: "These men are throwing our city into confusion, being Jews" (v. 20). Anti-Semitism was widespread in the Roman world; Acts 18:2 records that Emperor Claudius expelled all Jews from the city of Rome. That might explain the attitudes of the men who dragged Paul and Silas to the magistrates. God in His marvelous plan chose two men of just the right background so that even the scorn and abuse heaped on them would lead to the saving conversion of others.

### D. The Pretense (vv. 20–21)

#### 1. Of causing chaos (v. 20)

The first charge brought against the two missionaries was, "These men are throwing our city into confusion" (v. 20). Paul and Silas were accused of causing total disorder and chaos in Philippi, which in a sense was true.

#### 2. Of committing a crime (vv. 20–21)

". . . being Jews, and are proclaiming customs which it is not lawful for us to accept or to observe, being Romans."

Cicero, Tertullian, and others wrote of a law that said no Roman could follow the teachings of any religion that had not been approved by the Senate. Rome encouraged emperor worship. Some other religions were tolerated in order to keep peace among conquered peoples, but all worship had to be approved by the Senate, and Christianity didn't have that approval. That's why Paul and Silas could be accused of violating Roman law. It was a kangaroo court, a mob scene, a lynching.

Never restrict your gospel boldness for fear of persecution, or you will miss new opportunities for reaching people. Persecution simply translates your boldness into a new opportunity. In Acts 4, Peter and John were thrown in prison for preaching, which gave them the opportunity to evangelize the Sanhedrin.

The Sanhedrin threatened them if they continued preaching, but the apostles did continue, and more people were saved. The Lord blessed their boldness. Satan has yet to learn the foolishness of imprisoning a Christian. Persecution of Christians only ends in victory for Christ.

### E. The Pummeling (vv. 22–24)

1. The indictment (v. 22)

a. By the multitude

"The crowd rose up together against them . . ."

Mobs are unthinking, mindless, easily incited by someone lighting an emotional fire under them—and then they get furious without knowing why.

b. By the magistrates

". . . and the chief magistrates tore their robes off them and proceeded to order them to be beaten with rods."

Roman magistrates were accompanied by lictors, who functioned as enforcers or policemen. Lictors carried at all times a bundle of hard rods that included an axe—the axe for capital punishment, and the bundle of rods to flail lesser offenders. The magistrates commanded that Paul and Silas "be beaten with rods." Paul received that specific treatment at least three times in his life (cf. 2 Cor. 11:25), among countless other abuses he endured for Christ.

## 2. The imprisonment (vv. 23–24)

"When they had struck them with many blows, they threw them into prison, commanding the jailer to guard them securely; and he, having received such a command, threw them into the inner prison and fastened their feet in the stocks."

The jailer was unsympathetic toward Paul and Silas, but he was simply doing his job. He locked them in the filthy, dank inner dungeon, and in stocks. These were not the kind that existed in early America—a simple device that closed on a person's hands and feet. Archaeologists found that the stocks in Paul's day had a series of holes for the purpose of stretching the prisoner's legs to the extremity, to induce excruciating cramping. Paul and Silas had already endured a terrible beating with the bundled rods, which would have horribly damaged their backs and potentially caused internal hemorrhaging, damage to internal organs, smashed vertebrae, broken ribs, or even death. Then they were pushed, aching and bleeding, into the fetid darkness and further torture of the stocks, confined in filth and far from light or air.

## F. The Purpose

All of that just to preach? Couldn't they have avoided this mess, so they wouldn't injure themselves and preoccupy the other saints? But the reason Paul was so effective in doing the Lord's work was because he was abandoned to the cause. He had no thought for himself. He presented Christ to people, heedless of possible negative consequences. Most of us are the opposite; we evangelize carefully, so as not to offend, which makes us slow to preach Christ.

Paul didn't mind suffering for doing what was right. When he later wrote to the Philippians from jail, he said, "I want you to know, brethren, that my circumstances have turned out for the greater progress of the gospel" (1:12). In Philippians 4:22, he said, "All the saints greet you, especially those of Caesar's household." What was he doing while in prison? Winning soldiers to Christ. He also said, "Even if I am being poured out as a drink offering upon the sacrifice and service of your faith, I rejoice and share my joy with you all" (2:17). In Galatians 6:17, Paul said, "I bear on my body the brand-marks of Jesus." If Paul was injured, imprisoned, or even killed in ministry, he could still be happy because it was for the sake of Christ. He could be reckless because he was expendable, and he was pursuing certain glory and joy in Christ.

## II. SINGING PRAISES (ACTS 16:25–29)

So much of handling persecution is an issue of attitude. It's unlikely any of us has suffered as Paul and Silas did. But notice their attitudes in the midst of their suffering.

### A. A Spirit-Filled Attitude (v. 25)

"But about midnight Paul and Silas were praying and singing hymns of praise to God, and the prisoners were listening to them."

Paul and Silas couldn't sleep, given the circumstances. Instead, they talked to God for a while, and they sang praises—they continued witnessing to their fellow prisoners. They may have sung the Hallel, which is Psalms 113–118, or perhaps the early church had some hymns.

1. The perspective on praise

This is a crucial point of confusion in the Christian life for so many. It's easy to ask what those missionaries could possibly praise God for—on what basis could they do it?

The answer is simply this: God never changes. If God is worth praising in good moments, He is worth praising any moment. His praiseworthiness is not contingent upon your trouble.

In Philippians 4:4, Paul wrote, "Rejoice in the Lord always." He didn't say, "Rejoice in your circumstances." In fact, Paul testified, "I have great sorrow and unceasing grief in my heart" (Rom. 9:2). The Christian can say, "God, I don't know what this is all about, and it sure hurts, but I know You're on the throne, and I love You, and I praise You for what You're doing."

## a. Illustrated in the Old Testament

The prophet Habakkuk illustrates how the believer can be defeated when he begins to focus on his problems. Habakkuk was confounded by his serious questions about God's nature and plans, until he turned to fix his gaze on the unchanging God rather than on his temporal turmoil.

Even Christians can be prone to ask, "Where is God in my present trouble? Has He forsaken me?" But that is allowing circumstances to define God in your thinking. He hasn't changed. Be patient in adversity, and wait; God is perfecting you (1 Pet. 5:10). We read and recite and memorize Romans 8:28, but how many of us live like we believe it?

## b. Illustrated in the New Testament

Just before His crucifixion and ascension, Jesus told His disciples that while "sorrow has filled your heart" (John 16:6), "you will grieve, but your grief will be turned into joy" (v. 20). He likened the acuteness of their coming troubles to birth pains in that the very anguish that brings a laboring mother such pain also brings her joy once the child is born.

The believer's attitude is not to be, "Well, these are bad circumstances, but I'll get good ones later." No. The very circumstances that cause the pain will issue the joy—because of the pain's ultimate result.

The Christian life is completely shaped by your knowledge of God. A proper perspective of God puts everything else in proper perspective too. Most people derive their theology from their situations; they form their opinion of God and what He's like by what they experience.

But Paul and Silas knew the truth. They were singing praises, even while they were in tremendous pain. They weren't focusing on their circumstances; they knew that God had a purpose for their imprisonment. They simply waited on God and praised Him while they waited.

2. The pattern for praise

Do you wish you could do the same? Ephesians 5:18–19 tells us how: "Be filled with the Spirit, speaking to one another in psalms and hymns and spiritual songs, singing and making melody with your heart to the Lord." Those are the fruit of the Spirit-controlled life.

Living Spirit-filled doesn't eliminate problems, but it gives the glory of enduring them with victory. Paul didn't let negative circumstances trouble his heart. In 2 Corinthians 4:8–9, he said, "We are afflicted in every way, but not crushed; perplexed, but not despairing; persecuted, but not forsaken; struck down, but not destroyed." How could Paul handle that? The answer is in verses 16–18: "We do not lose heart, but though our outer man is decaying, yet our inner man is being renewed day by day. For momentary, light affliction is producing for us an eternal weight of glory far beyond all comparison, while we look not at the things which are seen, but at the things which are not seen; for the things which are seen are temporal, but the things which are not seen are eternal." In times of trouble, Paul looked to the eternal God.

## B. A Sovereign Act (vv. 26–29)

### 1. A supernatural event (v. 26)

"And suddenly there came a great earthquake, so that the foundations of the prison house were shaken; and immediately all the doors were opened and everyone's chains were unfastened."

God uses various means to grab the sinner's attention, but He is always effective. This event always excites me because it reminds me that when I share Christ with others, God is on my side, and He will move the earth, if need be, to accomplish His work of salvation. You're never alone when you evangelize. When the proper time comes for God to reach someone's heart through you, God will arrange events to prompt that person to open his heart. Some Christians have amazing testimonies about how different things worked together to lead to their repentance. No one yet was ever saved by accident.

So this very localized earthquake was strong enough to cause all of the jail's doors, chains, and stocks to open! God not only actively protects His saints, He actively makes them and their ministry effective. Live and work knowing that God is on your side.

2. A subsequent encounter (vv. 27–29)

a. Attempted suicide (vv. 27–28)

1) The jailer's assumption (v. 27)

"When the jailer awoke and saw the prison doors opened, he drew his sword and was about to kill himself, supposing that the prisoners had escaped."

The earthquake woke the jailer—there's no indication the other townspeople ever noticed it—and found all the prison doors opened. He immediately assumed that all inside it would have fled. He took out his short sword, the soldier's personal weapon, to kill himself.

2) Paul's assurance (v. 28)

"But Paul cried out with a loud voice, saying, 'Do not harm yourself, for we are all here!'"

Paul shouted to the jailer from the darkness not to kill himself. Imagine how shocked the jailer must have been to find that none of the prisoners had escaped! Why didn't the other inmates leave? God kept them all there; perhaps they had become attached to Paul and Silas, or they were too scared to escape. They had heard the apostles' praises and then felt the earthquake God sent.

b. Astonished submission (v. 29)

"And he [the jailer] called for lights and rushed in, and trembling with fear he fell down before Paul and Silas . . ."

God abruptly reversed the jailer's relationship to the apostles, from his treating them as lowly prisoners to now kneeling before them, trembling. Salvation is a sovereign work. Just as He did with the jailer, God sovereignly prepares each believer's heart to receive Christ by showing them their need for Him.

## III. PREACHING SALVATION (ACTS 16:30–32)

### A. Exemplified

The real excitement at this part of the story is that we get to see how God works salvation in a sinner's heart. We just explain to people how to become saved; He does the work of saving.

1. The desperation of the jailer (v. 30)

"... and after he brought them out, he said, 'Sirs, what must I do to be saved?'"

The jailer didn't ask, "What happened?" or "Why didn't you escape?" His mind wasn't on the earthquake; he was in the greatest crisis of his life. God had convicted his heart, and even if he didn't fully understand who God was or the way of salvation He'd made, the jailer knew he was a lost man who needed to be saved.

2. The declaration to the jailer (vv. 31–32)

a. The way to the Lord (v. 31)

"They said, 'Believe in the Lord Jesus, and you will be saved, you and your household.'"

The missionaries answered simply and clearly. In Matthew 19:16, a rich man asked Jesus a very similar question: "Teacher, what good thing shall I do that I may obtain eternal life?" He maintained that he had kept the whole law in obedience to God (v. 20). So Christ said, "If you wish to be complete, go and sell your possessions and give to the poor, and you will have treasure in heaven; and come, follow Me" (v. 21). Jesus wasn't saying that that act is salvific; He was telling the young man that his money was a barrier to his total faith in Christ. The Roman jailer had had all such barriers removed. He just wanted the way of salvation pointed out to him. So he desperately asked, "What must I do to be saved?" Paul and Silas answered, "Believe in the Lord Jesus Christ."

b. The Word of the Lord (v. 32)

"And they spoke the word of the Lord to him together with all who were in his house."

They first communicated that salvation is by believing in Jesus Christ, then they taught the jailer and all in his house who Jesus was and what He did. Paul and Silas's presentation of Christ was very simple because the way of salvation is very simple.

## B. Explained

1. The nature of saving faith

Salvation comes by believing in Jesus Christ, and there is no salvation apart from faith in Christ. Belief in Christ is all, as John 1:12 states, "As many as received Him, to them He gave the right to become children of God, even to those who believe in His name." Acts 2:38–39; 4:12; 11:13–17; 13:38–39; and 15:11 all confirm that salvation is through Christ. Romans 3:21–22, "Apart from the Law the righteousness of God has been manifested, being witnessed by the Law and the Prophets, even the righteousness of God through faith in Jesus Christ for all those who believe"—salvation is by faith alone; law or works can contribute nothing. Ephesians 2:8–9 says, "By grace you have been saved through faith; and that not of yourselves, it is the gift of God; not as a result of works, so that no one may boast."

2. The content of saving faith

Some people claim belief in belief, or that they have faith in faith. That is ridiculous. No belief but belief in Christ will save—Jesus Christ is Himself the content of the gospel.

a. You must believe who Christ is

John 20:31 says, "These have been written so that you may believe that Jesus is the Christ, the Son of God; and that believing you may have life in His name." Belief in Christ means you believe that He is who He claimed to be and that He can give life.

b. You must believe what Christ did

In 1 Corinthians 15:1–4, Paul said, "Now

I make known to you, brethren, the gospel which I preached to you . . . by which also you are saved, if you hold fast the word which I preached to you, unless you believed in vain. . . . That Christ died for our sins according to the Scriptures, and that He was buried, and that He was raised on the third day according to the Scriptures." In order to receive salvation, you have to believe that Christ died for your sins and that He rose again. Romans 10:9–10 says, "If you confess with your mouth Jesus as Lord, and believe in your heart that God raised Him from the dead, you will be saved; for with the heart a person believes, resulting in righteousness, and with the mouth he confesses, resulting in salvation."

So salvation comes by believing that Jesus is who He said He was.

## CAN SOMEONE ELSE BELIEVE ON YOUR BEHALF?

God had uniquely prepared the Samaritans to receive Philip's message by giving them the necessary context to understand it. Unlike the Samaritans, or many Jews still today, most Gentiles you encounter will not understand the importance of the statement, "Jesus Christ is the Messiah." Some people are more prepared than others to receive Christ, so be ready to explain the basics of who God is, what sin is, and what God's plan for the ages is. Give them the simple gospel, and be ready to answer their objections and questions. But most of all, remember that it is God who prepares the soil of men's hearts to receive the gospel, and that you must be ready to introduce them to Christ wherever or however you encounter them.

---

## IV. SEEING THE PRODUCT (ACTS 16:33–34)

When you preach the gospel to hearts ready to receive it, God gives blessed results. According to the end of verse 34, the jailer's whole family was saved. This was the formation of the church in Philippi—the uniting of the little group of women now with the jailer and his family.

Jesus said in John 15:16, "I chose you, and appointed you that you would go and bear fruit, and that your fruit would remain." In other words, "I want you to be productive." So did the jailer's fruit remain? Was he really saved? We have four reasons to think so:

### A. His Confession (v. 33)

". . . and immediately he was baptized, he and all his household."

Romans 10:9 says, "If you confess with your mouth Jesus as Lord, and believe in your heart that God raised Him from the dead, you will be saved." Belief in Christ is a matter not just of believing in your heart but also of willingly, publicly confessing Him as Lord. The jailer and his family were all immediately baptized, which is a public declaration of their commitment to Christ.

## B. His Compassion (v. 33)

"And he took them that very hour of the night and washed their wounds . . ."

The jailer went from not caring about their welfare to personally washing their wounds. The formerly hardened, totally unsympathetic jailer had been transformed in Christ. Jesus said, "By this all men will know that you are My disciples, if you have love for one another" (John 13:35). The jailer showed that his salvation was real through his love for Paul and Silas. Maybe you experienced that sudden love for other Christians when you became a believer. First John 5:1 says, "Whoever believes that Jesus is the Christ is born of God"—that's how you are saved—"and whoever loves the Father loves the child born of Him." If you really love God and Christ, you will also love other Christians. If you say that you are a Christian but you don't love your brother in Christ, then you are a liar (1 John 4:20). Paul said in 1 Thessalonians 4:9 that God Himself teaches His own to love one another.

## C. His Hospitality (v. 34)

"And he brought them into his house and set food before them . . ."

The jailer did just as Lydia had earlier (v. 15): He showed Paul and Silas hospitality. "If a brother or sister is without clothing and in need of daily food, and one of you says to them, 'Go in peace, be warmed and be filled,' and yet you do not give them what is necessary for their body, what use is that? Even so faith, if it has no works, is dead, being by itself" (Jas. 2:15–17). The best test of genuine, living faith is its loving action for others. Good works issue from true faith.

## D. His Rejoicing (v. 34)

". . . and rejoiced greatly . . ."

Just prior to this, the jailer was ready to kill himself. Now he was rejoicing with his family, Paul, and Silas. Only God can transform a man that quickly. There is no question the jailer had become a believer.

# V. SECURING PROTECTION (ACTS 16:35–40)

Paul's great concern was always believers' welfare. As he knew he was leaving Philippi, he thought of how to protect and care for the young believers he'd be leaving there. God had a plan for that also.

## A. The Dismissal (v. 35)

"Now when day came, the chief magistrates sent

their policemen, saying, 'Release those men.'"

The magistrates thought they'd put Paul and Silas through enough that they'd quietly leave town and cause no more bother.

## B. The Defense (vv. 36–37)

"And the jailer reported these words to Paul, saying, 'The chief magistrates have sent to release you. Therefore come out now and go in peace.' But Paul said to them, 'They have beaten us in public without trial, men who are Romans, and have thrown us into prison; and now are they sending us away secretly? No indeed! But let them come themselves and bring us out.'"

Roman law forbade especially corporeal punishment of a Roman citizen without due process. But it was God's plan that Paul and Silas shouldn't raise that defense at the outset so that they would evangelize all in the jail and the jailer's house. Now, though, Paul exerts his and Silas's rights as Roman citizens.

## C. The Dismay (v. 38)

"The policemen reported these words to the chief magistrates. They were afraid when they heard that they were Romans . . ."

### 1. The shock

The news that Paul and Silas were Romans frightened the magistrates because they knew they had violated Roman law by beating citizens. That endangered their own positions. So they feared Paul—enough that they continued to leave him alone the next time he returned to Philippi (cf. Acts 20:1–6).

2. The safety net

The magistrates' fear of Paul was good for the believers in Philippi. God used their association with Paul to protect that little group of believers. Paul also left Luke in Philippi to care for the church there, and God's sovereignty is again evident in the fact that Luke and Timothy were not imprisoned alongside Paul, because they weren't Roman citizens like Paul and Silas were. How carefully God orders everything!

## D. The Departure (vv. 39–40)

". . . and they [the magistrates] came and appealed to them, and when they had brought them out, they kept begging them to leave the city. They went out of the prison and entered the house of Lydia, and when they saw the brethren, they encouraged them and departed."

The city officials came to the prison and pleaded with Paul and Silas simply to leave. But the missionaries' main concern then was those new believers' welfare, so they remained long enough to see and minister to them all again before they left, having secured their protection.

That is how the complete cycle of evangelism works: Paul and Silas began by suffering persecution for the gospel, and they labored to the point of securing the new believers God had brought to Christ through them. Throughout, their message was the simple gospel they preached to the Philippian jailer: "Believe in the Lord Jesus, and you will be saved" (v. 31).

# FOCUSING ON
# THE FACTS

1. What does man seek, universally? How do people pursue that outside of Christ? What can happen when their pursuits disappoint them?

2. Describe how the church in Europe began and how Satan immediately launched his counteroffensive. What does that tell us about his methods for attacking the church? What might that tell us about how he is working against the church now?

3. Explain what this study of Acts has revealed about how Paul approached preaching. What was his outlook on suffering for the gospel? Describe his mindset and how he arrived at it, referencing other portions of Scripture to support your answers. Be sure to discuss both persecution and praise.

4. Walk through various passages of the Bible to explain the believer's relationship to suffering. How can you have the same attitude as Paul and Silas?

5. Explain the jailer's conversion. What is the message of salvation, and how did Paul and Silas present it to the jailer and all his household? What two fundamentals must a person believe about Christ to be saved? Support your answers with Scripture.

6. What proofs did the jailer give that his salvation was genuine? How did God, through Paul, protect the new Philippian church in their city?

## PONDERING THE
## PRINCIPLES

1. Read 2 Chronicles 15:1–15; Jonah 3; Matthew 3:1–6; Acts 8:5–6; and Acts 13:16, 43. How do those passages show people responding to preaching? What would have happened if the preachers in those instances had been too scared to preach? What will be the consequences, both for you and for unbelievers, if you refrain from sharing Christ with them? You have the answer to man's universal question: "What is the meaning of my life?" Consider today ways that you can preach God's glory to those who do not yet know Him.

2. Meditate on Paul and Silas's time in the Philippian jail. What was the likely impression they made on their fellow prisoners? How do you see their commitment to the Lord even in how they chose to leave Philippi? Write out the names of both the Christians and the unbelievers that you encounter frequently. Consider how and what you testify of God to each person on your list, especially in hard times. What kind of changes would you make? Read and pray through Philippians 4:4–8.